Shameless Persistence

Terri Hubbard

www.terrielizabethhubbard.com
https://www.facebook.com/pages/Terri-Hubbard-
Ministries/316684011788441
terrihubbard@gmail.com

ISBN-13: 978-0615938875
ISBN-10: 0615938876

Table of Contents

INTRODUCTION

What keeps you up at night? Have you ever wanted something so profoundly that the very thought of living without it made you dizzy? Have you ever had a longing, a void that's like a persistent but unreachable itch? Yearning to be scratched, only to be scratched and still no relief? Are your desires embedded so deeply within you, that seemingly you cannot reach them? And are these desires, thoughts and dreams so completely larger than you, that you know that they could have only been deposited in you by God?

If you answered yes to any of those questions, this book is just what you've been looking for. *Shameless Persistence* examines the account of the Canaanite women in Matthew chapter 15. It is about a woman who would not be denied, refused to be discouraged and in the face of everything negative, refused to quit until she got what she needed and wanted. This is *shameless persistence,* and this my friend is what you and I must have if we are going to realize the greatness that God has for us and break into our preordained destiny. *Shameless persistence* **is** about that inner something that won't let you quit or give up even when everything in you wants to. *Shameless Persistence* examines the dynamic of the kind of faith it takes to please God, and the persistence, *shameless persistence* it takes to walk into your destiny. This expose is raw, in your face, truth. It's not sugarcoated or pretty, the Canaanite woman's situation was not pretty, it was the ugly, awful reality that she called her life. She lived every miserable moment of it day after day. *Shameless Persistence* is not for the faint of heart. But if you can identify and allow the words on these pages to bless your heart, you will too like the Canaanite woman lay claim to the ultimate prize, your miracle.

Shameless Persistence is about finding and fulfilling your passions no matter what the cost, no matter how big the struggle. You cannot and will not be denied. My prayer for you when you put this book down is that your inner fires will be stoked. If you were fading, you now have a giant second wind, if you had lost sight of the possibilities; you now have a new vision, if you thought there was no way out, you now see an open door.

Be driven to your dreams! Be shameless in your persistence!

WOMAN WITH A PLAN

Then Jesus went thence, and departed into the coasts of Tyre and Sidon. And, behold, a woman of Canaan came out of the same coasts, and cried unto him, saying, Have mercy on me, O Lord, thou son of David; my daughter is grievously vexed with a devil. But he answered her not a word. And his disciples came and besought him, saying, Send her away; for she crieth after us. But he answered and said, I am not sent but unto the lost sheep of the house of Israel. Then came she and worshipped him, saying, Lord, help me. But he answered and said, it is not meet to take the children's bread, and to cast it to dogs. And she said, Truth, Lord: yet the dogs eat of the crumbs which fall from their masters' table. Then Jesus answered and said unto her, O woman, great is thy faith: be it unto thee even as thou wilt. And her daughter was made whole from that very hour. Matthew 15:21-28

Imagine yourself in the birthing suite of your local hospital. It's been almost twenty-four hours since you went into labor. The day before you start experiencing labor pains, and soon after, your water brakes! This is the day you've been waiting on for the past nine months. Since the day you tinkled on the end of the pregnancy test applicator and saw the + sign, indicating that the results were positive and that you are pregnant. Fast forward some 260 or so days and here you are in the birthing suite! Every thing's a go. No complications of any kind. All your OBGYN visits have been smooth, not as much as a hiccup. You're completely prepared. The nursery's been painted; you've bought and assembled the crib, hung curtains with images of little babies floating on pillowy clouds. Your baby shower was awesome, you received everything you need to take care of your little bundle of joy. Bottles, diapers, blankets, burp cloths, bassinet and car seat. Everything is ready. Now your cervix is dilated to nine centimeters, and the contractions are 40 seconds apart. Your breathing is short and spasmodic, the horrific labor pains, unbearable, but none of that matters now. The baby is almost here! Finally you hear the words you've been waiting for, *push,* and in the midst of agonizing screams with one great p-u-s-h, it's all over. She's here! In your arms lays the most beautiful, perfect little human you've ever seen. Your precious, wonderful baby girl.

You're in awe when you look at her for the first time. A head full of beautiful black ringlets framing the softest buttery most flawlessly chubby face. Beautiful brown eyes, ten perfect fingers and ten perfect toes, the cutest most bitable little button nose, absolutely undeniably the most perfect beautiful baby you've ever seen!

Now fast forward 12 years. The same beautiful big brown eyes are now cold and silent, staring mindlessly into space. The black ringlets that were once framed the bright bubbly face are pulled and twisted, matted and smelly with bits of trash and dried food strewn throughout. The once flawless perfect complexion now marred by self-inflicted scratches, welts and scars.

This used to be your baby, it still is, but this is your baby now, helplessly tormented by a devil. By day your daughter cowers in corners running from the light of the sun as if her body is being poisoned by its rays. And by night, she roams from room to room unable to sleep, taunted by an unseen entity. Every attempt to touch her results in violence, even the lightest stroke of her hair causes her to erupt in a barrage of profanity and fighting. Your heart breaks each time you look at her. You berate yourself each time, secretly wishing she would die. You don't know how much longer either of you can live like this.

Now you have some idea of the dilemma facing the woman in the 15th chapter of Matthew. Now you have an idea of what it takes to get to the place of *shameless persistence.* By the time this Canaanite woman got her nerve up to approach the Master, she had already experienced so much hell; it never occurred to her that she could experience anything even remotely crazy enough for her to leave without getting what she came for. She had come to a place where living without her miracle was not an option. As painful as her life was now, facing the future without deliverance for her daughter was even worse. We've all heard the term 'rock bottom' well this was her rock bottom. And like this woman, you can't really find that place until you are ready, until life and circumstances make you ready. You have to be beyond sick and tired, you must be *shamelessly* sick and tired. When you're shameless, you don't care what anybody says or thinks about you or your circumstance, you're ready. And that's the place where miracles thrive, and where *shameless persistence* is rewarded. This is actually the kind of faith that pleases God.

For the purpose of our story we'll call the Canaanite woman Sara. Sara had taken as much as she could; the exhausting ritual of parenting a child tormented by a devil had taken its toll on her. I can imagine beyond the sheer smothering pressure of trying to maintain some level of sanity in her home, she had to endure the stares and stinging gossip of her neighbors. Why did it happen? Was it her fault? Could she have done something to protect her daughter? All these questions and more swirled around in her head as she made her way to the stranger she had heard so much about. Would he help her? Or would he send her away without her miracle? She wouldn't let herself think about that now, she was a woman on a mission and she refused to be denied. This was a once in a lifetime opportunity. This Jesus, the one they call the *Miracle Worker* was right in her back yard! There was no time for fear, no time for doubt; the time was now to take her daughter's healing!

IGNORED

And, behold, a woman of Canaan came out of the same coasts, and cried unto him, saying, Have mercy on me, O Lord, thou son of David; my daughter is grievously vexed with a devil. But he answered her not a word. Matthew 15:23

Have you ever been ignored? Have you ever been talking to someone and they just turned their back and walk away from you? Or have you ever been speaking and after you have said your peace, the person looks at you like you were speaking a foreign language they couldn't understand, and *then* they walk away from you like you weren't even there? Being ignored, dissed, or excused, incites a special ire. Your first emotion is laced with *how dare you, I don't believe they had the nerve to....* Sara the Canaanite woman no doubt had the same thoughts. Ignoring or dismissing a person suggests that what you have to say is of no value to the person you are addressing. Although that might actually be true, common courtesy dictates that we at least acknowledge that we *heard* what was said. But this was not the case with Sara and Jesus.

Our story begins as Sara cautiously navigates the mountainous country that lies between Tyre and Sidon, beginning her journey early that morning just before dawn. Her woolen tunic wrapped around her head and shoulders, shielded her from the early morning chill. Her feet are bound in leather sandals and a leather water bottle hangs from her waist. Sara doesn't know exactly how long her journey will take, but she is prepared to travel a significant distance if that's what it takes. Finally after several hours of traveling mountainous, rocky terrain, she approaches a growing crowd of people. Surely this is the crowd that is following Jesus, the *Miracle Worker*. Inside the ring of people standing around him, he is surrounded by the twelve men that always accompany him, and just beyond them she can clearly see Jesus, the man who has been credited with giving sight to the blind and straightening withered limbs. Surely he has something left for her. Slowly she inches closer, not too close or fast as to appear brazen, but not too far back as to appear indifferent. She pushes her way through the crowd of folks "Excuse me, please let me through, I must get through, please excuse me." She ignores the stinging retorts coming from the crowd as she finally bursts through the crowd and stands facing the object of her quest, Jesus. "Excuse me Sir." The barely audible words slipped from her trembling voice. No response. Sara swallowed the dry lump in her throat, (the vision of her demonically tormented daughter forever tattooed in her mind) reminds her of the reason she's standing before him. She clears her throat and with boldness and volume she calls to the *Miracle Worker* again. "Have mercy on me, O Lord, thou Son of David!" Pausing momentarily as he turns to look in the direction of this proclamation. "My daughter is grievously vexed with a devil." The words tumbled out. She'd said it. Now she held her breath as she waited for him to do respond to her request. Surely he would say a few words, command something or wave his hand and voila', or something? Then her daughter would be healed! But to her dismay, nothing happened. Did he hear her? He had to have heard her she reasoned. He looked right at her, his piercing eyes locking onto hers, commanding her attention, but he said nothing. Seconds that seemed like centuries passed as she held her breath waiting for the stranger to speak. Surely he was about to pronounce her daughter's healing. Surely now he would call her to him and tell her that everything would be all right. With bated breath, Sara waits and waits, and waits. Then without saying a word, he turns and looks away from her without so much as even a nod. Wait a minute. Sara's heart drops, her knees weak. *Did he not see me?* She wondered incredulously. What just happened? Isn't this the part where this Jesus, this *Miracle Worker* is supposed to acknowledge my request? Sara stood stunned. Maybe he didn't hear me. She reasoned.

But he looked into my eyes! He had to have heard me. But....nothing. Not one word! Not even a syllable! Sara couldn't understand. It didn't make sense. For one split second her heart sank.

He ignored me. Just walked away without as much as a nod of recognition. But just as quickly, her heart reminded her of what she left at home. The very thought of her daughter's dead lifeless eyes, haunted by an unseen force, the unseen force that had stolen her baby away from her, steeled her resolve. She would not go back home without getting what she came after. She wasn't leaving. Ignored or not, she wasn't leaving, it wasn't over. She wasn't going to let it be over. Maybe he did hear her, maybe he didn't, and maybe he didn't understand she needed something more than just eye contact. Whatever the case, it didn't matter. If it meant she had to stand there all day, she didn't care. She would do it. Heels dug in, she made up in her mind. She wasn't leaving without getting what she came for!

Sara didn't know it but she had just passed her first test. She didn't know it but her faith was being tested. Jesus wanted to know just how much her daughter's deliverance meant to her. But Sara passed with flying colors! She had been ignored by the one and only Jesus Christ, The King of Kings, Emmanuel, God in the flesh! But she wasn't moved. She didn't flip, she didn't trip, she didn't even flinch. There was something deep down inside of her, a determination so strong, that even when she was ignored by the very God of the universe, she didn't stagger when he turned his back to her. A lot of people, dare I say most of us would have been discouraged and went home fussin' and fumin'. We would have been highly offended and stomped off mad and empty handed. It would sound something like this, "Oh no He didn't!? Or "I know he did not just look at me and turn his head away! I know he heard me call him, I even called him 'Son of David', I could have just said hey Jesus, but no, no I went all the way, showing him all kinds of extra respect!"

I am persuaded that most of us would have left that day empty handed. We would have forfeited the miraculous all because we perceived that Jesus didn't respond to us the way we assume he should have responded to us. Sound familiar? Have you ever felt in your hour of greatest need Jesus wasn't there for you the way you *think* he should've been? If this thought has ever crossed your mind, you are not alone. We humans have the tendency to get caught up in our own whirlwind, and when we do, it's kind of like when we are children. We cannot see anything but *our* problem and *our* solution. That might have been the case in another scenario, but Sara wasn't about to let her emotions get between her and her miracle. She tucked her feelings in and kept it movin', if she was offended by being ignored we'll never know, she didn't show it. She just kept it movin'. And that's just what we need to do. Keep it movin'. Not bad advice. But sadly offense is one of the greatest tricks of the enemy. We get so caught up in our own pride; we don't realize the enemy just stole what was rightfully ours. Satan says "poor you, he didn't make over you and your problem like he should've. Don't you have a right to your miracle? Your deliverance is just as important as anybody else' he's delivered?" So now your feelings are hurt, and you have the right to your feelings. After all, didn't God make you with these feelings? Watch it. This is a set-up. Yes absolutely we were made with feelings, and sometimes things do not go our way or the way we think they should go, but so what? Just because you don't have your answer today doesn't mean that you won't get it. Remember it ain't over until God says it's over. Besides, which would you rather have your bruised hurt feelings, or your miracle? This part of Sara's story is reminiscent of the story of Naaman the leper in *2 Kings 5:1-14 (KJV.)* Naaman was called a man of valor, he was a popular well thought of commander of the army of the king of Syria, and it was through him that God had given victory in battle to Syria. Naaman had it going on; he had wealth, fame and position. Long story short, Naaman was all that and a bag of chips. But as great as all this sounded, Naaman was a leper, and that wasn't cool. Leprosy was and is an infectious incurable disease. Or at least that was the case until Naaman encountered the God of Israel. Leprosy starts as small red spots on the skin that progress into large white scaly spots. As they spread all over the body, hair, fingernails and toenails weaken and fall out. This progression leads to fingers and toes rotting and falling off. Even the gums of the infected person shrink and their teeth fall out. Finally the nose, eyes, arms and other body parts rot and fall off. This of course leads ultimately to death, a slow painful, agonizing death. Certainly this shouldn't be the end of the story for a great warrior like Naaman, but unfortunately there wasn't a cure for leprosy. But fortunately there was and still is a God to whom leprosy is nothing. In your spare time you should read the whole story of Naaman, but for now I will just give you a quick summary.

Naaman's wife's servant told her of a prophet in Israel who if Naaman was around, could heal him of this terrible disease. Now I can imagine this news thrilled Mrs. Naaman because I'm sure she wanted a healing for her husband about as much as he did. So she tells her husband. And Naaman is so excited about what he hears, he in turn tells his master, Ben-Hadad II of Aram, king of Syria. Now the king of Syria gets so excited by this great news that he tells Naaman, "you get started on your way, and I'll send a letter to Joram, king of Israel". It was similar to a letter of recommendation. So Naaman headed on down to Israel, with the letter and ten talents of silver, six thousand shekels of gold and ten changes of clothing. In today's economy that was more than 1.2 million dollars! Naaman really wanted his healing bad. And he was willing to put his money where his mouth was, and so was the king. There was just one problem. When Naaman arrived with the letter, Joram, the king of Israel flipped. The problem was the king of Syria; Ben Hadad had in the letter told the king of Israel, Joram that he, the king of Syria was sending Naaman to *him* personally to heal Naaman. Now the king of Israel knew that he didn't have power to heal anybody, least of all this Naaman, so he thinks the king of Syria is trying to pick a fight with him. He was so upset that he ripped his clothes off his body. In ancient times, when someone ripped their clothes off, it was bad news. So when the prophet Elisha heard about it, he sends word to the king of Israel for Naaman to be sent to him. Once Naaman was at the Prophet Elisha's house, he tells him what to do to get his healing. He proceeded to send word by his servant, Gehazi, for Naaman to go and dip in the Jordan River seven times and his skin would be restored. Now this is where the miracle would be received or forfeited! Naaman didn't like the fact that the prophet did not come himself and speak to him but sent a messenger. I guess Naaman thought because of his who he was, being famous and wealthy etc., the prophet should have come to him personally and perhaps waved his hand over the leprosy and healed him. But he didn't, and Naaman got an attitude. He was offended. Not only didn't he like the fact that he had been instructed by Elisha's messenger, Gehazi, but he apparently didn't like the prophet's or God's method of deliverance. The Jordan River was not clean enough for him, if he just had to dip himself in water, why couldn't he dip in the Pharpar or Abanah rivers in Damascus? He was so mad he actually left in a rage, headed back to Syria, leprosy and all. This just wasn't working out the way he thought it should be working. And had it not been for his quick thinking servant, Naaman, the leper, would have stayed Naaman the leper. But thankfully his servant was able to convince him that he was getting caught up in the *details*. Naaman was about to miss his miracle over minor details. His feelings were hurt, he wasn't saluted by the prophet as the great and mighty Naaman, he was sent to the river that wasn't the cleanest. Details all details! And petty ones at that. Seems silly doesn't it? But this is an extremely successful tactic of our enemy Satan. If he can get us to concentrate on the small stuff and get us caught up in our own pride, he can steal our miracle right out from under our nose! But we can learn a lesson from Naaman and Sara, feelings come and go, they are about as stable as water. Never have and never will be dependable. We can be happy one minute and a few minutes later we remember what so-and-so did to us, and get angry all over. Don't get bamboozled by your feelings. Trust me, they will change. But your miracle? Now that's another story. Miracle opportunities don't come around every day, so when you have a chance at one don't miss it. If it means you have to swallow your pride and suck in those hurt feelings, so be it. Just remember, those feelings won't hurt so much when you are dancing for joy at your answered prayer! Sara the Canaanite woman was officially ignored, and not just ignored by Joe Average guy, she was ignored by the one and only Emmanuel, God in the flesh.

This has special significance for several reasons. Obviously given the severity of her daughter's condition, Sara realized this was not a case for just anybody. And I'm sure she did as any mother would do, she sought help from the finest minds of her time. So she knew that only a miracle, a supernatural intervention would suffice. So imagine how excited she was when she found out that this *Miracle Worker* was in her backyard! I can imagine how I would feel. Finally a realistic shot at having a normal life!

As a mother of two girls and three dogs (yes I love my canines like that!) I am at my wits end when they have an upset stomach or a head cold. As long as they are sick, I am in sympathy with them in their sickness. If I had my way, my children (nor canines) would ever experience any discomfort at all so when I think of Sara, I can only imagine how she felt when she thought now there was a chance her daughter would be cured. I can imagine the moment she heard about a man performing miracles, hope swelled within her. She heard about all the great happenings in Israel, just across the border from her, you know how news travels. No doubt she heard the story of the Centurion's servant. The boy was at the brink of death, but at the word of Jesus he was healed (*Luke 7:1-10*)! She probably heard the story about the man, who had a demon and was tormented, just like her daughter. Somebody told her Jesus, this *Miracle Worker*, was in the synagogue teaching one day and all of a sudden this possessed man in the crowd started heckling him, shouting "why are you bothering us, Jesus of Nazareth. Have you come to destroy us demons? I know who you are; you are the Holy Son of God." About that time Jesus heard enough, he told the man to shut up and commanded the evil spirit to come out of him. And it did (*Luke 4:31-37*). And then she heard there was the woman who had been hemorrhaging for twelve years. This woman had been to doctor after doctor to get healed, spent every dime she had and still wasn't cured. But all that changed the day she found the *Miracle Worker*. Sara was impressed by this woman's faith. She had taken all she could and even though it was against the law for a bleeding woman to be in public, not to mention touch someone who was of the ministry, Sara heard this woman crawled on her knees through the crowd and sneakily touched the hem of his robe. Sara didn't know all the particulars, but she heard that the woman received her healing (Luke 8:43-43.) Wow! Just one touch of this Man's clothes! There had to be something wonderfully powerful about this man, if just touching his clothes healed her. She didn't know just what it was, but she was determined that she was going to find out.

So now this was Sara's moment. That same *Miracle Worker* that she'd heard so many stories about is standing right in front of her. And she asked him for her miracle...and he ignores her! Now there are several possible reactions that Sara could have had at this point of this story. I want to point out the reactions that will *not* get you the desired results. First, you do not want to respond with "I know he didn't' just ignore me!" This response is identified by the trademark neck/eye roll, hand on the hip, sucking of the teeth, and the look of incredulity. Now just to keep it real, I must confess, this is probably the most frequent response, I myself have participated in this response several times. Something inside you just says, *who do you think you are?* Or even, *do you know who I am?* In truth this response is rooted in pride. Even if a request is a valid one, it can still be viewed as an intrusion, albeit a peaceful one. Anytime a request is made, the person making the request assumes four things; they assume they have a right to make their request, they assume their request can be granted by the one being asked, they assume the one being asked wants to grant the request and finally they assume they are entitled to a response. As you can see, all these assumptions are based on the beliefs of the one making the request. But why do they have the right to make a request? What makes them believe the request could be granted? And if the requests is granted then why? When you look at it from this angle, it changes things up a bit. It helps us to maintain a position of humility. Although we know our Father God wants us to approach us with our needs, it's still smart to proceed boldly yet humbly.

Secondly, this is not the time to hurl some smart remark and stomp off in a rage. Again referring to the previously mentioned assumptions, do you have the right to make a request? Assuming the person wants to grant the request are they able to? And are they required to make any response? This response too is rooted in pride. It places the needs and wants of the one making the request above the one to whom the request is being made. Even though we think at times are world is falling apart, and in truth it may literally be falling apart, does it mean our situation trumps anyone else? If we look at our example in a practical way, Sara, our Canaanite mother, didn't know anything about Jesus other than what she heard. He could probably heal her daughter but she didn't know if he had his own agenda for that day. She didn't know if he would want to help her. She didn't know if he would require her to do something herself before he would help her. She just didn't know, so it really wasn't smart to go running off in a huff. She didn't have all the facts. She didn't know all the angles. And as the story unfolds, this move by Sara proves to be part of the key to getting her miracle.

Thirdly, this is not the time to pout or cry. First no one likes a crybaby. And this too is rooted in pride. It screams "I wanna' have my way!" to which anybody could scream back, "well who are you?" Crying and pouting are like cheating on a test. Its success is based on an unfair advantage. If I cry or pout, I may be able to manipulate someone into getting what I want. Manipulation can be very dangerous, although this tactic would have never worked on Jesus, sometimes desperation causes us to consider it as a viable opportunity. Not. Manipulation is one of the most heinous examples of pride. It suggests I'll do whatever I have to do to get what I want! Godly shameless persistence is just that, Godly. We never have to stoop to worldly or man induced tactics to get what God has already designed for us to have. I don't know how Sara the Canaanite knew that, but she did. And that leads us to the right response to being ignored.

Humility. It is so easy for us to let our fleshly desires control us. We all struggle with areas in our life that just seem to be out of control. For some it's addiction, for others it's unforgiveness, for others it might be jealousy. Pick your poison; we all have an Achilles heel. And as long as we live in this garment of flesh, we will have one. Hopefully we will not be fighting the same battle over and over, but rest assured we will have a battle to fight. And it seems that the lack of humility or pride; is an ongoing battle for many. But Sara our example got it right. She was so smooth. I'm going to paint this picture for you using my Holy Spirit imagination. Sara is absolutely broken. Raggedy and pushed to the edge by a demon possessed daughter, she swallows the miniscule thread of pride she thought about having, and exposes herself unabashedly, crying, no, wailing moans from the innermost part of her being. At this point, she's down on her knees begging a man she doesn't know to help her. I pause here to put this into perspective for you. Can you imagine yourself, at your wits end, probably looking like you could be an extra in a horror movie, approaching a total stranger and asking them to save your life? This was Sara. It wasn't a pretty picture. She wasn't in her Sunday best. Her hair wasn't done, nails on point or make-up 'beat to the gods'. She was a wreck. Sara was at one of the lowest places that a person can get. She was begging from a stranger. And all she had was hearsay that this stranger could help her. But she got it right. At that moment, being ignored was the least of her problems. Being ignored was nothing compared to what she had been. Being ignored was a temporary problem, fixable. And she knew it. At that moment being ignored meant nothing to her. She had audience with the *Miracle Worker* and everything was going to be alright. She knew getting into this position was half the battle, and if this man Jesus was anywhere near striking distance, there was no demon, no distraction, no remark or lack thereof that was going to keep her from getting what she came for!

What if you and I had that same attitude? Something deep inside Sara knew being blown off was just a test. What about you? Sometimes God just wants to know how badly you want it. Sometimes he has to check our heart. He is our Father, he wants to give, however some would like him to be our 'sugar daddy'. The 'sugar daddy' seekers will soon get tired and fall away, but the true lovers of God are like the *Every Ready* bunny and a *Timex* watch, they just keep on going. Sara wasn't even thinkin' about givin' up. How far are you willing to go to get your miracle? Will hurt pride keep you from walking in your destiny, from walking in your dreams? From scratchin' that itch? I hope not. Learn a lesson from Sara. Swallow any pride you have. Humble yourself. Let it roll off your back like water. Nothing, I mean absolutely nothing is worth you missing out on God's best for your life.

PRIVATE PAIN, PUBLIC PANIC

But he answered her not a word. And his disciples came and besought him, saying, Send her away; for she crieth after us. Matthew 15:23

Let me continue sharing my Holy Spirit imagination of our example of Sara our Canaanite mother. The last we see of Sara, she is on her knees begging at the feet of Jesus. Having made a complete public spectacle of herself, crying and begging at the feet of the *Miracle Worker*, only to be ignored by him. Now you might think that this was a small insignificant happening, but the truth of matter is that wherever Jesus appeared, crowds even multitudes of people followed. That was actually the reason he was in the coasts of Tyre and Sidon. He needed to get a break from the crowd. But....guess what? That was not going to happen. So imagine with me, Sara is on her knees in a heap on a dirty mountainous road. Prostrate on her face literally before God and the citizens of the tiny coastal towns. She has been publically humiliated, begging at Jesus feet only to be ignored. And it doesn't end there. Now Jesus' entourage gets involved. They add their two cents "give her what she wants and get rid of her, she's making a scene!"

Now this time I want you to use *your* imagination. Can you see yourself there instead of Sara? Let me help you out. Imagine you in your most embarrassing situation, dress caught in your underwear, toilet paper hanging from something, mumbling to yourself when you thought you'd hung up the phone only to have the party on the other end hear everything you just said about them. Need I go on? Thought not. Now imagine your most embarrassing moment magnified by a gazillion! Bad enough Sara had to debase herself and come to Jesus in the first place. At least at home she didn't have the world looking at her, but now she's in public, been ignored, *and* now a group of men she doesn't know have joined the conversation.

"Send her away, she's making a scene and getting on our nerves!" I can imagine Sara was horrified. Have you ever attempted to do something on the low, (secret) only to be busted big time? The only good thing about Sara being called out was that these strangers were actually on her side. They were making some noise trying to get her some help. This was Sara's next test. She had some noisemakers, a cheering section. Somebody else involved who was on her side. Now I'm sure, Sara wasn't making all these moves consciously, but we can learn a lesson about how to receive what you need and want, and not go away empty handed. Every one of us is going to have a time in our lives when we are facing what seems to be our biggest battle. And sometimes we think we have to handle the situation all by ourselves. Unfortunately we don't always realize that keeping our mouth shut or refusing to get anyone involved (in our *business*) can really be a tactic of our enemy to set us up for defeat. Remember the story of Bartimaeus in *Mark10:46-53*? The account goes like this; Jesus was leaving Jericho with his disciples and a large crowd of people were following him, because you know everywhere he went, Jesus always drew a crowd. The account goes on to say that a blind man, Bartimaeus, was sitting by the side of the road begging. Now when Bartimaeus *heard* Jesus was coming, he started yelling. Now I want to pause and make a point here. Bartimeaus couldn't *see* anything; he had to rely on what he heard. And obviously he'd *heard* something about Jesus. He had to have heard that if he needed a miracle, this Jesus was the one that could perform it. Just like Sara. The account goes on to say that as soon as Bartimaeus started yelling, '*thou son of David, have mercy on me*' begging for help, someone in the crowd told him to shut-up. I'd like to pause again here and make a few more observations. First, the nerve of whoever that was that told Bartimeaus to shut-up! What was it to them if Bartimeaus was making some noise to get Jesus' attention? Who appointed them the crowd control police? Jesus had his own security staff, I'm sure if he needed any help, he had it. Secondly, isn't there always someone around trying to rain on your parade? Always someone trying to keep you from getting what you need, just like they tried to keep Bartimeus from getting what he needed. Sounds just like you-know-who, Satan, the enemy. John 10:10 tells us the thief comes to kill, steal, and destroy, and he's always got one of his minions positioned near us trying to steal our breakthrough and our miracle. But not this time. I like Bartimaeus' moxie. Instead of getting quiet, he got louder! He flipped the scrip on the haters in the crowd. And that's just what you have to do sometimes to get your miracle! Change it up on the haters. You know who they are, we all have them even God has some haters (*Rom 1:30*) they're everywhere. But the next time someone tries to shut you down, make some noise. Act like you have lost your mind! The more the enemy oppresses you, the more you should call out to Jesus. Open your mouth, use your weapon! *Psalm 34:15* says, the eyes of the LORD *are* upon the righteous, and his ears *are open* unto their cry.

Now about the haters, I do not believe Bartimaeus was the only one in that crowd who needed something from Jesus, but I do believe he was the only one who wasn't afraid, or ashamed or too proud *to get* what he needed. He wasn't afraid to make a scene or causing a ruckus if it meant he would get his sight. Haters for whatever reason, pride, jealousy, envy, ignorance or just plain meanness, don't want to see anyone else blessed. And they sure don't want you to come out of your struggle. But isn't that just like the spirit of the enemy? If haters aren't hatin', they're feeding you some garbage about how *you're not going to make it this time. This time things are different. You brought this all on yourself, made your bed now lay in it.* Job had his haters too. In his lowest moment, his 'friends', Eliphaz, Bildad and Zophar, came to encourage him. Eliphaz believed that Job was suffering because of some kind of sin he had committed. And Bildad and Zophar believe that in some way Job had actually offended God. Zophar goes as far as suggesting that whatever Job was suffering was not even *close* to what he deserved! Are you kidding me!? Even if Job was guilty of these things, I doubt true friends would rub his face in it. With these kinds of friends, Job sure didn't need any enemies. Word of caution! If you have *friends* like Job's friends *run*, don't walk to the nearest exit. Get away from them as soon as possible! Bartimaeus was in the company of people like this, but he didn't let the haters steal his miracle. Haters want what you want, but don't want to do what you will do to get it. Bartimeaus too was shameless in his persistence. He didn't care who heard him or saw him. He didn't care if he was making a spectacle of himself. Bartimaeus yelled at the top of his lungs "Son of David have mercy!" That got Jesus' attention and he stopped in his tracks! And something miraculous always happens when Jesus stops in his tracks! Sometimes it takes some persistence and sometimes it's instantaneous. But make no mistake when you get Jesus' attention, something is *going* to happen. Jesus was moved by Bartimeaus boldness and his persistence. He called Bartimaeus to him, and when the crowd saw this they went from hating to celebrating. This brings me to another point I want to address. There's always someone monitoring your success and generally this is a good thing. Yes there are haters, but there are also those that are rooting for your victory, and that's another reason why staying on task and getting your miracle is imperative. First and foremost it brings glory to God when our deliverance comes. Secondly, our success encourages someone else to hold on. If we can make it, they can make it. And finally it builds our faith. As long as we live we will be fighting battles. We go from victory to victory. Every time we come through one rough situation, it strengthens us for the next test. We learn the character and nature of our God through each storm we go through.

Bartimeaus made a scene, but he got the attention of Jesus, and Jesus asked him what he wanted. Jesus, God in flesh, asked Bartimaeus, a blind beggar what he, a blind beggar, wanted! How amazingly incredible is that? The God of the universe, the creator of everything, the Word made flesh, asks a poor, blind man, what can I do for you? I don't know about you, but that is so phenomenal, it really staggers the mind when you think about it, and all because Bartimaeus made some noise and didn't care who knew it. Bartimaeus got somebody on his side, he got his cheering section. They might have been made up of haters, but even the haters had to rejoice when Jesus called him. *Matthew 22:44* does say the Lord will make your enemies your footstool. Bottom line, Bartimaeus can never be called blind again, he got just what he wanted, he used to be blind, but after his encounter with Jesus, he could see. And can you imagine all the things that changed for him? Aside from being able to see and enjoy things he never could before, he didn't have to beg anymore! He could get a job and support himself. He could find a wife and get married, start a family, become a productive member of society. Instead of being a beggar, he was now the one who could be a blessing, his whole world changed, all because he wasn't afraid. What could you do if you weren't afraid? What is it that you need from God today? Are you willing to do what it takes to get his attention? We can learn a lesson from those who got their miracle, Bartimaeus made a move, got the crowd involved, got the attention of Jesus. Got results. Sara, our Canaanite woman did the same thing! She made some noise and got cheering section. Although she still didn't get the response she was hoping for right away, it kept her in the game until she did! Make a noise (pray) go for broke (no fear) expect your miracle!

THE WORD SPEAKS

But he answered and said, I am not sent but unto the lost sheep of the house of Israel. Matthew 15: 24

Last we saw of Sara, our Canaanite mother, she was surrounded by the citizens of Tyre & Sidon, the disciples and Jesus. Even though she still hadn't received the miracle she had come for, slowly things were starting to shift in her favor. Now Sara had someone else on her side. The disciples were Jesus hand-picked ambassadors. The responsibility would fall on them when Jesus completed his assignment and returned back to the Father. So you would think when they backed you up it would carry some weight with their Leader. I'm sure Sara thought so too, but let's remind ourselves of what has transpired so far.

Our story started when Sara approached Jesus and asked him to help her daughter who was seriously possessed of the devil. This was her first encounter with him. From the results she got, being ignored by the *Miracle Worker,* it looked bad. But as we noted earlier, she wasn't easily discouraged. Then she got some help. Jesus disciples were on her side. They pleaded her case, not really for her, but because she was drawing attention to them. At this point, I'm sure Sara's faith soared. But just as it started to soar, it was dashed again. This time Jesus did respond, but it still wasn't the desired response she was looking for. But he did respond. Now we're talkin'. It wasn't exactly what she wanted to hear, but it was more than she got the first time. Hope was building. There was light at the end of the tunnel! I can just imagine she thought within herself; *at least I got a response this time!* This brings us to a critical point. Even though you don't get what you wanted or expected the first time, there is still hope that you will. Have you ever heard the saying, *as long as there is breath, there is hope?* I believe one of our main problems is that we give up way too soon. Sara kept pressing. All she had was a word; all she needed is a *Word.* The word of God declares that '*faith cometh by hearing,*

23

and hearing from the word of God. Sara staked everything she had on what she heard. She didn't have the bible, the scriptures don't record there had been any conferences or conventions in her neighborhood. All she had was a *word*. A word from someone, who knew someone, who heard about someone, whose great auntie's neighbor heard about something that happened.... But the fact remains, all Sara had to go on was a word. The word kept her moving. When we are *shamelessly persistent,* you must have an unshakable foundation built on the word, and not just any word, the Word of God. Let's pause and chew on this a while. *John 1:1* says; *In the beginning was the Word, and the Word was with God, and the Word was God.* And verse fourteen goes on to say; *and the Word was made flesh, and dwelt among us, (and we beheld his glory, the glory as of the only begotten of the Father,) full of grace and truth.* Sara our Canaanite woman was looking at the Word made flesh! She had a word that lead her to *the* Word! The scriptures give us insight to how powerful the word of God is. *Hebrews 11:3* tells us; *through faith we understand that the worlds were framed by the word of God, so that things which are seen were not made of things which do appear.* The worlds were created by the spoken word of God! *Genesis 1:3* says; *and God said, Let there be light: and there was light.* Light appeared at the command of God! Sara was standing in the presence of God, the Word that became flesh, the same God that spoke the worlds into existence! Do you understand how powerful this is? I don't know if she was aware of *whose* presence she was in, but she knew one word from this man would change her life! She knew one word from him was more important than anything else in the world! *Psalm 138:2* is one of my personal favorite scriptures. It says; *I will worship toward thy holy temple, and praise thy name for thy loving kindness and for thy truth: **for thou hast magnified thy word above all thy name**.* This scripture tells us that the word of God is bigger than anything else, even his name! Do you get that? His word is more important than his name!!!! And we know that the name of Jesus isn't just any ordinary name, Jesus is the name above every name! *Philippians 2:9-11* says; *God had highly exalted him (Jesus) giving him a name that is exalted above every name and that at his name, (Jesus) every knee would bow and every tongue would confess that Jesus is Lord.* Here's another way to understand how powerful the word of God is, Bro. Keith More of More Life Ministries, Branson Missouri explains it along these lines. "The word of God is so powerful and so awesome that if he would ever lie, the worlds would cease to exist, because the worlds and everything else is held together by the awesome *power* of the word of God!" Sara was standing on the verge of receiving life changing, earth-shattering, deliverance bringing word! And she wasn't going anywhere!

Dear readers, I am convinced that once we make up our mind to receive what God has promised us, a whole new hoard of satanic minions is unleashed against us. The proclamation of faith from our lips is like blood in the water to a shark. They are drawn to it. And the evil one is drawn to you when you proclaim your faith. But when we arm ourselves with the word from God, we become more than conquers, we become invincible, we become unstoppable! That's why the word of God is so important. God's word is unfailing. It has to do just what God sends it to do. It cannot fail! *Isaiah 55:3* declares; *so shall my word be that goeth forth out of my mouth: it shall not return unto me void, but it shall accomplish that which I please, and it shall prosper in the thing whereto I sent it.* Whatever God's word is ordained to do will be done as long as we are obedient and follow in his plan for our lives. *Hebrews 6:18* tells us that it is impossible for God to lie, so if he said it, that settles it! Sara held on by faith to a word she heard. I don't know how she knew about faith, but I do know that somehow faith rose up in her and she refused to be denied her miracle! Faith mixed with the word makes us unstoppable! Faith is that force that propels you forward when you don't see a way out. Faith is the force that won't let you quit. It's the ingredient we mix with the word, that causes us to receive our miracle. And faith is an integral ingredient in *shameless persistence*. And here's why; faith pleases God (*Hebrews 11:6*). Our faith makes God happy. It brings him pleasure to know that in the face of every adversity and every impossibility, we will still believe in him. And did you know that bible says that to God, the trial of our faith is more precious than gold? I believe we bring a special joy to the heart of God when we believe his word, even when everything we see is contrary to what he says. That brings us back to blood in the water. Satan hates us;

and when we determine in our minds, that we are going to stand on God's word, he's determined that we will not be successful. Another reason our faith pleases God is because the evil one always wants to make our God look small and suggest that he is incapable of doing what he said he would do. So every time we have a faith test, he tries to defeat us. He tries his best to make us doubt God's word. Think about Adam. Picture it. Indescribable beauty all around. Perfect climate. No need for clothes or shoes or air-condition, or coats. Peace and tranquility. And a wife who I believe was drop-dead gorgeous. Absolute perfection! Cue Satan. All Adam had to do was to *keep* the garden, replenish the earth and keep his hands off of the tree of knowledge of good and evil. That's all. Pretty easy. But....The evil one sees an opportunity to discredit God's word. He says three little words to Eve; *hath God said?* In other words, *did God really say that?* In Eve's heart, that was just enough to undermine the credibility of God's word and she was swayed by Satan's suggestion rather than standing on God's word. And guess what? He's still using this tactic today. If he can make us believe God's word is ineffective, he can convince us that it is a waste of time to trust what he says. Abraham also had a word from God. He was told that in his old age, he would have a son (*Genesis 17:15*). Seemed impossible, Abraham was ninety-nine and Sara was ninety, but God gave his word to Abraham, and he simply cannot lie. But because of the impossibility of the circumstances, Sara didn't believe God's word. But God is still faithful. Abraham did have a son, Isaac. Sara's faith might have faltered, but Abraham stood strong. And we must stand strong too. Just know that God and his Word are inseparable. He is his Word (*1 John 1:1*).

FROM DESPERATION TO DELIGHT

Then came she and worshipped him, saying, Lord, help me.
Matthew 15:25

The scriptures don't tell us much about Sara the Canaanite woman, but one thing's for sure; she was no dummy nor was she a quitter. Sara was a worshipper! This act of submission, this worship changed a seemingly hopeless situation, into basically a sure fire guaranteed miracle. Again with the help of my Holy Spirit influenced imagination, I can see Sara on her knees, in the midst of a crowd of onlookers, some jeering, some making fun of her, some probably annoyed for whatever reason, maybe some thought she was blocking their opportunity, but in spite of all this, she's not deterred. She's already been ignored probably laughed at, someone's probably saying, why doesn't she just give up, go home, stop making a fool of herself! But none of this moved Sara. She wasn't leaving without getting what she came for. And suddenly, down on her knees, before the King of Kings, something strangely wonderful happens. She begins to worship. Can you imagine? In the midst of all this craziness, she begins to open her mouth and bless God?! True worship is one of the most selfless and humble acts we can participate in. And probably *the* reason Sara received her miracle.

Let's analyze this in detail using ourselves as the example. Like Sara, we need a miracle. We understand that at this point no one can help us, no one but God. We are fully aware that we have exhausted all of our efforts, and there is absolutely nothing more we can do. This fact alone makes us incredibly uncomfortable. No one wants to think that they are helpless. It goes against our grain. We all want to be self-sufficient, but in truth we were made to look outside ourselves for help. So here we stand helpless. I don't know about you but my first instinct is to cry. For me it is literally painful when I realize that I have come to the end of my ability. First I cry, then I pout, then I get angry. Sara could have done all these things, but incredibly she worshipped! She could have been so consumed with her feelings and given into them, but she worshipped! Sara made a conscious decision to worship. News flash, *Worship is not automatic.* In *Psalm 34:1* David says; *I will bless the Lord at all times.* He had to *make* himself bless and worship God. His flesh didn't feel like praising, but he went beyond his feelings and made himself worship. How many times have you and I given in to our feelings? It is *so* easy. We can do it without trying, it comes natural. But what if we worshipped? The act of worship is beyond special. It is the most wonderful gift that we can offer to God. This selfless act requires us to abandon every ounce of pride and fear, trusting that our worship, our complete openness will be accepted. At this point we are truly, ultimately at the end of ourselves, exposed, naked, and vulnerable. I can imagine Sara, her bone weary body lying at the feet of Jesus. Her once pristine garment covered with the dust of the well-travelled dirt road. Prostrate at the feet of Jesus. Begging for the life of her daughter pleading for his help, then somehow her desperation transitions into delight. Something clicked and she was no longer worshipping because she was afraid, sad and desperate, but now she was caught up in her worship. No longer did she need to worship, she *wanted to* worship! The scriptures do not tell us what all was involved in her worship, for there are many acts that comprise the act of worship. Sometimes worship is combined with singing or lifting of the hands, sometimes it is accompanied with shouting or dancing. I can imagine Sara kneeling at the Master's feet, her hands extended touching even caressing his feet as she lovingly pours her worship on him. Not unlike Mary who wiped the feet of the Master with her tears, I imagine Sara weeping softly as she whispers Holy Spirit birthed words of adoration and praise (because true worshippers can do so only through spirit and truth). *Holy Master, Sweet Rose of Sharon, Precious Son of David, Thou Lamb of God, how wonderful you are, there is no one like you, I worship, I praise you, you are the Healer, you are the Miracle Worker, there is none like you, there's nothing you can't do. I bless you, I adore you, I honor you. Lord help me!* We don't know how long this went on, we don't know exactly what was said, we don't know what position she was in. All we know is that her worship, sweetly and freely given moved the heart of God. And that is the ultimate reward, moving the heart of God. She crossed the threshold into pure and perfect worship. Have you ever experienced this? Is that a desire you have? Do you want your worship to so bless the Almighty that it becomes something special to him? God is drawn to those who worship him. I want everything I do, to draw him to me. I want to worship and praise so that he knows he has a special invitation to dwell in the midst of my worship. Worship is the key to your miracle. So the next time you feel you are stretched beyond the breaking point, open your mouth and worship. Don't complain, don't rehearse the circumstances, just open your mouth and bless God. Do it even if you have tears streaming down your face. Do it if you have to scream out in pain in between every word. Worship God as if you've lost your mind! Ignore everyone and everything around you! They don't know what you need and even if they did, they are powerless to do anything about it. For those of you who might not know how to start, let me help you. Worship in its simplest form is magnification. Start by just thanking God. Thank him for whatever comes to your mind. Thank him for the small things, thank him for the big things, just thank him. It doesn't matter what for, there's no special formula. As you continue to worship, begin to remind him of his goodness! Remember and recall how he has lavished his love on you! Acknowledge his greatness and his wonderful acts! Sing praises to him; begin to dance in his presence! Worship and keep on worshipping. Don't stop! Don't quit! I promise that soon you will transition from desperation to delight. Sara was the living embodiment of *Psalm 37:4* 'delight thyself also in the Lord, and he shall give thee the desires of thine heart'. Sara found the answer. And you will too. The more you worship, the more you will *want* to worship. So refuse to be denied! Worship until you move the very heart of God and like the Canaanite woman, God will visit your worship, and he will give you the desires of your heart too!

WHATEVER IT TAKES

But he answered and said, It is not meet to take the children's bread, and to cast it to dogs. Matthew 15:26

"Take the children's bread and cast it to the dogs?" Sara's precious pure worship finally brings the first direct words from the Master specifically directed to her. At last she's on the brink of her miracle. Almost to the finish line, one more hurdle. Jesus finally speaks, he acknowledges that there is indeed help available but not for her, she's a dog. She was in fact not a covenant child, and therefore the 'bread', the covenantal promise of healing, was not available to her. Sara was a Gentile, and Gentiles were not the people of covenant. All Gentiles were considered dogs. Now unfortunately for probably any other person on the planet, the chance of obtaining a miracle would have stopped here. On a good day, if we're trying really hard to follow Jesus, and stay in the realm, we can ignore being ignored. And on a really good day after we have just completed a season of prayer and fasting, we *might* be able to ignore the haters and the hecklers. *But,* how many of us would have endured all that Sara endured, haters, hecklers, walking for miles in the hot sun, over rocky terrain, the crowd, the stares, the whispers, only to finally get to Jesus and then be called a dog? Now mind you, the terminology he used for dog is translated 'little dog' a term more of endearment rather than disgust, but a dog is a dog. And I don't know too many people who would let that comment, endearing or not, ride. I know of many fights that have broken out for far less than calling someone a dog. If you read my book *Lessons from a Four-Legged Life Coach,* you know I love dogs, my four-legged babies sleep in the bed with me! They are my heart and as much as I love them, I wouldn't want to be called a dog. And as much as I love them, I know they are dogs, not people. They sniff everything, putting their noses and mouths everywhere, including among other things, each other's private parts! I can dress Jazzy up all day long in pink ribbons and bows, even put a little tutu on her, but I guarantee you, if given the chance, she will roll in the grass or pick up some unidentified animal part lying on the side of the road. Love her with all my heart, but she is a dog. I can safely say no one wants to be called a dog, even from Jesus. But he called Sara a dog. But once again, she didn't flinch. Let's use our Holy Spirit inspired imagination, imagine Sara's first thoughts, *finally he acknowledges me, but he tells me that I don't qualify for his help because I'm not like him.* Instant heartbreak. I can imagine her the entire morning, spent travelling to an unfamiliar place, where she *heard* she could find Jesus, finally she gets there, fights through the crowd, gets close enough to ask for help, gets ignored, gets heckled, asks for help again, only to be told help is available, but she doesn't qualify. That pretty much sums it up. I don't know about you, but honestly at this point, there was a time in my life where I would have probably given up. But there is a wonderful little scripture in *Proverbs 24:10.* The Message Bible says it like this; *if you fall to pieces in a crisis, there wasn't much to you anyway.* When I'm feeling a bit overwhelmed by life's crisis, this scripture 'jabs' me back in line. I believe the reason we have the account of Sara in the bible is to encourage us to *never* give up. She could've quit, obstacle after obstacle, one roadblock after another, she must have thought, *how much can one person take?* I don't know if you've ever experienced anything like this in your life, but I have, and it's not a fun place to be in. Often when we are experiencing difficulty, like extended test and trials, God has us in a time of preparation.

Let's look at the example of Joseph as recorded in Genesis chapters 37-50. Joseph was Jacob's favorite of twelve sons and all of his eleven brothers knew it and hated him for it. Jacob loved Joseph so he even made him a one of a kind designer coat. Now under different circumstances, this wouldn't have been a problem, but when you have eleven other kids standing around thinking *where's mine?* It does have a tendency to stir some stuff up. And if this wasn't enough to make Joseph the most hated member of the family, his dad Jacob also used him to keep an eye on his older brothers, sort of like a spy. If you didn't know better, you'd think Jacob was setting his son Joseph up for a beat-down! But in Jacob's defense, he had a special love for Joseph because he had him in his old age. The story of Jacob and Rebekah, Joseph's parents is a beautiful one. I encourage you to read it if you haven't, it will help you to understand why Jacob was so partial to his son Joseph. But I digress, back to the story of Joseph. Joseph was a dreamer and an interpreter of dreams. Now the bible doesn't tell us how many dreams he had, but it tells us about the two most important dreams he had. Joseph dreamed that one day his brothers would pay obeisance to him, in other words they would bow down to him. Poor Joseph, it's one thing to have a dream that pretty much tells you that your family at some point is going to be subservient to you, but to *tell* them about it is another thing, especially if you already *know* that they don't like you. Bless his heart, Joseph had no way of knowing that this would be the proverbial *straw* that would break the camel's back, but it did. From the moment his brothers heard this, the murderous seed of hatred was sown in their hearts, they wanted to get rid of the dreamer. And it wasn't long after Joseph shared his dream with his brothers/haters, they beat him, threw him in a pit and sold him as a slave. Now I'm not going to tell you all of the story because I really want you to read it, it really is a wonderful story, however I will tell you, the hatred his brothers had for him set in motion a chain of events that changed the course of history for Jacob *and* his family. Joseph's seventeen year journey from the 'pit' literally to the 'palace' showcases his perseverance, his *shameless persistence*. Can you imagine waiting seventeen years for a dream to come true? Joseph had so many opportunities to abandon his God given dream. He was thrown into a pit by his brothers; he was sold as a slave, falsely accused, imprisoned, and forgotten. He could have easily given up and derailed God's awesome plan for his life. But he held on through every awful thing that happened to him. He was shamelessly persistent in his commitment to stand firm. In every spiritual journey, there will be a time when our faith will be severely tested. I remember a few years ago I was going through my pit to palace experience.

In 2004, I went through the most devastating experience of my life, outside the loss of my parents. My husband and I loss everything we had due to a financial crisis. This crisis lead to foreclosure on all of our properties. Yes is said proper*ties*. At that time we had two houses and two parcels of land that we were getting ready build on. I remember the day the big orange moving truck pulled up in front of our house accompanied by the sheriff. He informed me that he had a court order that was being served, and that the moving company was here to carry it out. So I woke my kids and their overnight guest (they were having a sleep over), told them to get their clothes on. I got dressed, packed a few important papers and proceeded to watch as the moving company packed my things and my life up and carried it all away to storage. I remember my neighbors sharing their sorrow because they didn't know we were moving and they were going to miss us, what they didn't know was that I didn't even know that I was moving! We left our house that day and moved in with my mother for what I was sure would be no more than a few weeks. Well a few weeks turned into six years! Although my mother's house was nowhere near a pit, quite the contrary, my girls had their own room and my husband and I stayed in the guest room, it just wasn't home, and we all know there's no place like home. (I talk about this part of my journey at length in *Lessons From a Four-Legged Life Coach, Volume 2*) Looking back now, I know that the six years spent in my mother's house was a time of preparation. While I was going through it, it felt like a time of great trial. Actually it was both, it prepared me for where I am right now in my life, and my faith was tested, for me and for God. For me because it made me know that with God's help, I can withstand anything, and for God, because now I know, he knows that I am ready to be used to be an instrument for him. I admit there were some days I felt like I was dying; it was a major effort just to breath. But I endured. Many days through tears, but I stood. Yes some days I was tempted to throw in the proverbial 'towel', but those were the days I learned how to be *shamelessly persistent*. I knew that if I could just hold on, a change was coming. I remember kissing the carpet, prostrate on the floor in prayer, praying many nights, and some nights *all* through the night. But I didn't care, I knew the only way I would make it through this season of testing was to draw even closer to God, and that I believe, is his ultimate goal in *allowing* us to be tested. So it was with Sara, I believe Jesus was allowing this situation to prove her faith. And like her, our faith muscle must be tested. You will never know how much faith you possess, until it is put to the test, remember it's only after our faith is tried in the fire that we come out as pure gold!

YES, YOU'RE RIGHT BUT...HOW ABOUT OPTION B?

And she said, Truth, Lord: yet the dogs eat of the crumbs which fall from their masters' table. Matthew 15:27

The easiest way to diffuse a disagreement is to agree with the adversary. Sara was on point yet again. I am tempted to say that she was one smart cookie, but what Sara possessed was more than just your average street smarts, she was *driven*. So far she has had a solution for every obstacle and roadblock, and I believe it wasn't because of her own abilities, I believe this relentless determination; the *shameless persistence* that is inextricably tied to her destiny. And *destiny* is built into our spiritual DNA even before we are spoken into existence. *Jeremiah 1:5* says; *before I formed thee in the belly, I knew thee...* God knows everything about us even before we were born, to him, every day of your life journey is an open book. And he knew Sara would be a perfect example for us women to identify with, so he built *shameless persistence* into her DNA, so it wasn't just coincidence that she heard about Jesus and decided to seek him for her daughter's healing, it was her *destiny* to demand her daughter's healing! You see, this kind of destiny influenced persistence, is the kind that propels you forward even when everything around you says to quit. It propels you forward when *you* want to quit. All through scripture and even in life, we see example after example of people who have overcome insurmountable obstacles to snatch victory from the jaws of defeat. This was Sara. Once more she was met with yet another reason why she shouldn't have her request granted. But yet again, she didn't panic. Sara had passed the test of being ignored, harassed, heckled, called a dog, and told that she didn't qualify, BUT she finally was engaged in conversation with the King of Kings, and you just *know* something good was bound to come out of that conversation, and it did.

Once more Sara had her wits about her. She didn't disagree with what Jesus said, she accepted his summary of the situation, but she gave herself some wiggle room. She basically said, yeah you're right, but how about option B? Again it was *shameless persistence* at its best. She gave the Master something to think about. Sara agreed with him that she was a dog, but she also made her case as to why even a dog should be allowed to get something, even a crumb. Sara recognized even if she wasn't qualified for the complete and total package, couldn't she just get a little crumb? Smart very smart. Maybe you don't qualify for the 2.8 million dollar mansion, but you'll settle for the $750,000 custom build with all the upgrades. Maybe you don't qualify for the 21 day excursion through the south of France, but you'll take ten days in Maui. My point, don't give up. There is a little hidden jewel of scripture in Luke chapter 11, verses 8-11, the Message bible says it like this 'then he said, *"Imagine what would happen if you went to a friend in the middle of the night and said, 'Friend, lend me three loaves of bread. An old friend traveling through just showed up, and I don't have a thing on hand. The friend answers from his bed, 'Don't bother me. The door's locked; my children are all down for the night; I can't get up to give you anything. But let me tell you, even if he won't get up because he's a friend, if you stand your ground, knocking and waking all the neighbors, he'll finally get up and get you whatever you need.* The King James Version refers to this *importunity*. In other words be *shamelessly persistent*. Let's pause here and revisit what shameless persistence is, it is doing what you have to do, no matter what you have to do to get it done. Remember Sara endured the obstacles of shame, people, and prejudice. Joseph endured family hatred, being thrown into a pit, false accusation and imprisonment. For both of our examples it would have been so easy to quit. This same scripture tells us to ask, seek, and knock. All of these verbs are in the present participle, which means keep on asking, keep on seeking, and keep on knocking. Don't quit! Whatever happens, just don't quit. In my daughter Loria Dionne Hubbard's newest book, *The SSGG to: 35 Things Every Sassy Saved Single Girl Should Know!* She has a chapter called 'Have a plan z'. In other words, prepare to be prepared. Persistence is the key to your miracle!

SWEET TASTE OF VICTORY

Then Jesus answered and said unto her, O woman, great is thy faith: be it unto thee even as thou wilt. And her daughter was made whole from that very hour. Matthew 15:28

Finally! Sara heard the words she had been waiting to hear, I like the way the Message bible says; *Jesus gave in. "Oh, woman, your faith is something else. What you want is what you get!"* Right then her daughter became well! What you want is what you get! All her struggle, all her sacrifice, every cruel and hurtful insult, every sleepless and anxiety filled night, all the shame, all of the hopelessness, every dark and negative day, all of it, was finally over! Using my Holy Spirit inspired imagination, I can see Sara the second the words usher from the mouth of Jesus, scream with pure ecstasy. Her body collapses to the ground, every fiber of her being drained from the constant weight of her battle. Laughing and crying, rejoicing and praising, as the realization of victory settles over her. Finally it's over, her daughter is healed. I can imagine Sara lying on the ground, amazed, giddy, experiencing that 'pinch me' moment, then rising to her feet, she offers Jesus a simple thank you, then she turns and begins the long journey back home. I'm sure for Sara; the journey back home didn't seem as long as the journey to find Jesus. As tired as she must have been, I imagine her skipping, even running back over the rough mountainous terrain, running with tears streaming down her face. Running back to her daughter, the daughter who was once a lost soul, tormented and oppressed of the devil, now free and delivered. As a mother of two wonderful daughters, I can only imagine how Sara felt, no words could describe the moment she laid eyes on her daughter who was now healed of her oppression. Sara's faith fought for her, and now victory was hers.

Jesus said Sara had *great faith*; the very God of the universe was impressed with her *shameless persistence*. And as a result, her wish was his command. Will he say the same thing about your faith? Will you be shameless in your pursuit? Just remember when you come to the feet of Jesus, you will never leave empty.

HUFF AND PUFF....I'M STILL STANDING

I am convinced every word of scripture is God-breathed, incapable of failure and completely and utterly true. I also know that our enemy, Satan, knows and believes every word of God, and his ultimate goal is to make us doubt and disobey God. His pursuit is also relentless. But God's word reminds us that 'greater is he that is within us, than he that is in the world'. I want to encourage you to be shameless in your persistence no matter what. I know at times your struggle looks never ending. You may be struggling with health issues, with finances, with relationships or lack thereof, it might be anger, unforgiveness, or trust issues, whatever your battle, stay focused. No one ever said, it would be easy, even Jesus himself never told us the battle would be easy, but what he did say was that we could cast all of our cares onto him.

One day, my daughter Dionne and I were just rejoicing and praising God about some of the awesome things he's doing for us. We were shouting our praises and declarations of victory and refusing to be denied our God given and prepared destiny. We were pumped! In fact, I even had a 'pinch me' is this real moment? Fast forward twenty-four hours, we both were in the emergency room of our local hospital. We were in an automobile accident; thankfully no one was severely injured. Although no accident comes at a good time, this one really came at a bad time in my life. There were already things going on around me that commanded too much of my time and attention, the last thing I needed to deal with was an accident and its subsequent drama. I could feel the beginnings of a 'funk' trying to settle in over me. But I am learning, just breathe and stay calm and remember that in spite of what it looks like, God really is in control. As I contemplated the newest round of foolishness engineered by Satan, Holy Spirit brought to my mind the famous children's story, *The Three Little Pigs.* The long and short of the story is this; each pig built a house, one of straw, one of sticks, and one of bricks. The big bad wolf came to piggy number one's house of straw, threatened to huff and puff and blow his house in and eat him up, and he did. Then the big bad wolf proceeded to the second pig's house that was made of sticks, and threatened to huff and puff and blow down his house and eat piggy number two, and he did. On a roll, big bad wolf proceeded to piggy number three's house. He tried to do the same thing there, but piggy number three had a house made of bricks. All the huffing and puffing didn't do a bit of good, and in the end it was the wolf that ended up as dinner this time. What is the point to my throwback to nursery rhymes? Our setbacks and roadblocks are like the big bad wolf. How often has he told us that we're not good enough? It will never happen for us? That we're inadequate? We don't have enough? Lies all lies, don't listen to them. Often our challenges appear larger than they really are and they are always accompanied with fear and panic. But if we can remember that we are surrounded by the fortress of God's word that remind us that 'no weapon formed against us shall prosper' and 'lo I am with you always even until the end of the world' and 'the name of the Lord is a strong tower, the righteous run in it and are safe', we will always be victorious. So stand your ground, keep it movin' and be shameless in the pursuit of your goal!

SHAMELESS PERSISTENCE SMALL GROUP DISCUSSION QUESTIONS

1. After reading Shameless Persistence, what does that term mean to you?

2. Can you identify with our main character Sara? Why?

3. What principles about being shamelessly persistent did you learn from reading this book?

4. Do you have areas in your life where you can apply these principles?

5. How will you apply the principles that you learned?

6. Why do you suppose Sara's experience was so difficult?

7. Do you have any special scriptures that keep you focused during your difficult times? What are they?

8. How could you encourage someone else during their time of difficulty?

ABOUT THE AUTHOR

Terri Elizabeth Hubbard is a wife, mother, daughter, sister and friend. Married to her best friend of thirty years, Dewayne, together they pastor *Beulah Apostolic Church* in Mount Vernon Ohio. Terri is a gifted bible teacher, sharing the word of God and practical every-day living strategies. Terri travels extensively speaking at women's retreats, workshops and seminars. She is also the president and CEO of *Sistafriendzz,* an organization dedicated to meet the needs specific to pastor's wives, and Retreats International, a company that plans and operates retreats for religious, corporate, and personal clients. Terri is the proud mother of two daughters, Loria Dionne, who is also an author, and Daria Solomon who is the mother of Terri's grandson, David Elwood, and Corlaila Renee.

For more information or to contact Terri please visit her website @
www.terrielizabethhubbard.com
https://www.facebook.com/pages/Terri-Hubbard-Ministries/316684011788441
terrihubbard@gmail.com

Other books by Terri Hubbard:

Lessons From A Four-Legged Life Coach- 30 Minutes A Day With Your Dog Will Make You Healthy, Wealthy, and Wise

First Ladies Club

Books by Dewayne Hubbard Jr.

My First Book of A's

My First Book of B's

My First Book of C's

Books by Loria Dionne Hubbard:

The Single Christian: Your Sassy Saved Single Girl's Guide to Sex, Dating & Relationship A series of encouragement, life lessons and pure humor. VOL 1 2

The SSGG to: 35 Things Every Sassy Saved Single Girl Should Know

CPSIA information can be obtained
at www.ICGtesting.com
Printed in the USA
BVHW050524140223
658413BV00008B/707